DOWN THE DRAIN

THOMPSON YARDLEY

DOWN THE DRAIN

THE MILLBROOK PRESS • BROOKFIELD, CONNECTICUT

Cataloging-in-Publication Data

Yardley, Thompson.
Down the drain: explore your plumbing/Thompson Yardley.
Brookfield, Conn.: The Millbrook Press, 1991.
40 p.: col. ill; cm (A lighter look book)
Includes bibliographical references (p. 38)
Includes index.
Summary: Discusses the principles of household plumbing,
water supply, and personal hygiene.
1. Plumbing, house—Juvenile literature. 2. Baths—
Juvenile literature. I. Title. II. Series.
696.13
ISBN 1-878841-40-8 pbk.

First published in the United States in 1991 by
The Millbrook Press
2 Old New Milford Road
Brookfield, Connecticut 06804
© Copyright 1990 Lazy Summer Books Limited
First published in Great Britain in 1990 by
Cassell Publishers Limited
6 5 4 3 2

HAVE YOU HAD A BATH TODAY?

The best way to read this book is to begin at the beginning and read all the way through. You'll be amazed at what you'll find out:

What happens when water goes down the drain!
Why you have to wash!
Where water comes from!
How to make giant bubbles!

But if you want to read about one particular thing, such as soap or showers, look in the index at the back of the book.

Would the dirt build up on your skin so that after about twenty years you'd look like this?

Aargh!

It's a space monster!

Aargh! Run!

NO! But you might smell a bit! That's because very small creatures called bacteria live on skin and in dirt.

These creatures usually called germs. They can give off gases that smell quite horrible.

SKIN SHEDDING FACT

Your skin never stops growing. The outer layer keeps peeling off and takes the dirt with it.

Dead skin peels off in flakes that are often too small to see

BACTERIA GAS FACT

Bacteria in your intestines can produce about 1 quart (1 liter) of gas each day!

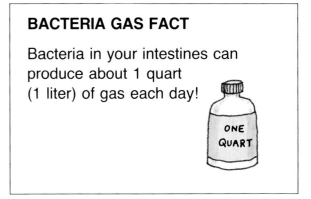

ONE QUART

BACTERIA

As well as bad smells, bacteria sometimes cause illnesses such as . . .

TETANUS! CHOLERA! TYPHOID! FOOD POISONING! DYSENTERY!

Some of these illnesses are caused by drinking dirty water.

Because harmful bacteria live in dirt, you have to wash off the dirt to get rid of most of them.

But they soon come back . . .

BACTERIA BABY-BOOM FACT
Bacteria grow very quickly. They can double in number every twenty minutes.

A single bacteria is called a bacterium.

Here's one bacterium left after washing.

After twenty minutes,

it splits into two bacteria.

After forty minutes,

they split into four bacteria.

After one hour,

they split into eight bacteria, and so on.

SOAP AND SKIN

Here's a common sort of bacteria . . .

They are so small that you could get more than a thousand into the space taken up by the period at the end of this sentence.

The bacteria shown at the left are called *streptococci*. They live in your intestines. If you don't wash your hands after using the toilet, streptococci can get into your mouth. Then you may get a sore throat.

Soap makes washing easier. But . . . not all types of soap get rid of all types of bacteria. Some bacteria will still be alive even if your skin looks spotless. But . . . don't worry. Your body can fight small numbers of bacteria. It's only when there are too many of them that you become ill.

Wow! I can still see a speck of dirt! I'll try something stronger!

AAARGH!

BLEACH DANGER FACT

Some chemical cleaners, such as bleach, are labeled "poisonous" or "corrosive." Something that is corrosive can damage your skin and other surfaces.

SOAP AND SKIN

Skin is the largest organ of the body. It keeps your insides in and the outside out!

People who scrub their hands too hard can damage the skin and get a rash. This is because the skin is protected by a thin film of oil that is easily washed off.

Below is a close-up of a bit of skin.

PUMICE STONE FACT

Pumice stone is a rough sort of rock found near volcanoes. It's used to scrub away stains on the skin. But . . . it can damage the skin, letting harmful bacteria in.

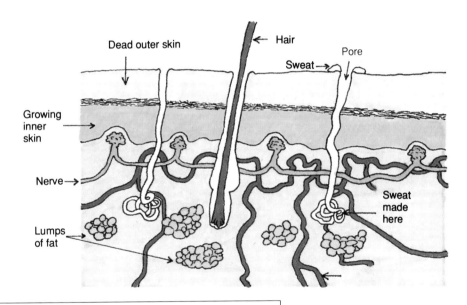

Dead outer skin
Hair
Pore
Sweat
Growing inner skin
Nerve
Sweat made here
Lumps of fat

Close-up of fingerprints before washing (enlarged side view of skin):

Close-up of fingerprints after washing:

Soap loosens dirt from the skin. It also washes away some of the dead skin, taking the dirt away with it. Notice how your fingertips feel smoother after washing.

HAIR AND FINGERNAILS

People used to brush their hair to keep it clean. This made it glossy and strong. These days people usually wash their hair with shampoo. This is quicker, but too much washing removes natural oils and can damage the hair. Most people don't need to wash their hair every day.

Dandruff isn't dirt. It's just flakes of skin from your scalp.

A BAD CASE OF DANDRUFF

Fingernails are great places for bacteria to live. You can spread bacteria all over your body when you scratch!

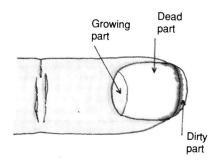

Only part of a fingernail is growing. The end that you cut off is dead. That's why it doesn't hurt when you trim it. The dead part is pushed out by the growing part.

The best way to clean dirty fingernails is with a stiff nailbrush.

TEETH

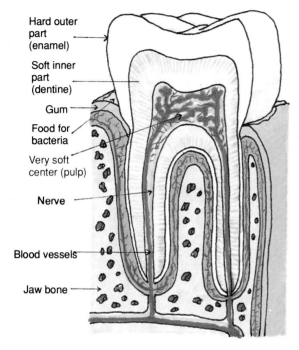

Hard outer part (enamel)

Soft inner part (dentine)

Gum

Food for bacteria

Very soft center (pulp)

Nerve

Blood vessels

Jaw bone

CLOSE-UP OF A TOOTH

Have you brushed your teeth today? Bad teeth are caused by tiny bacteria. The bacteria live on bits of food left on your teeth after eating. These bacteria give off acids that make holes in the hard surface of the teeth. Then the softer inner part soon rots away. Bacteria grow quickly on sugary, sticky food such as cookies and candy.

Older children and adults should have 32 teeth. Ask your parents how many bad teeth they've had taken out. You may be surprised!

It's a good idea to clean your teeth after every meal as well as before going to bed. Brush your teeth the way your dentist shows you. Brushing properly is much more important than the type of toothpaste you use.

Of course, if you're dirty all over, you'll need a bath or a shower . . .

SHOWER POWER

There are lots of different showers!

Here's one sort that people use.

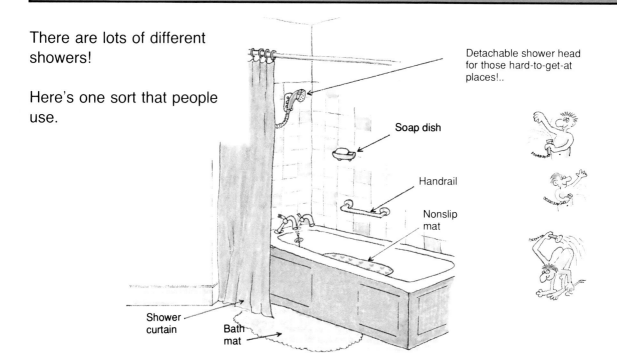

Detachable shower head for those hard-to-get-at places!..

Soap dish

Handrail

Nonslip mat

Shower curtain

Bath mat

SHOWERS OR BATHS?

Showers are much more healthful than baths. When you take a bath, the dirt stays in the water with you.

Soaking in the bath feels great, but showers use a lot less water.

TRY IT OUT!

Plug the drain. Take a shower and see how much water you used. Don't let the water overflow! Compare it with the amount of water you need for a bath.

ERK!

TO THE DOCTOR

TRY THIS SHOWERY TONGUE TWISTER!

SLIPPY SOAPY STEAMY SHOWERS CERTAINLY SAVE SOAKING SKIN IN SUDS!

Baths are shaped so that an adult can relax like this . . .

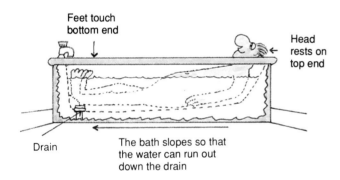

Feet touch bottom end

Head rests on top end

Drain

The bath slopes so that the water can run out down the drain

But . . . baths are too short to lie down in, so there's less chance of slipping under the water and drowning. Young people aren't so tall, so try not to doze off!

Check the temperature before you get in a hot bath! . . .

YOW!

WHAT TO DO IF YOU SCALD YOURSELF

Hold the scalded part under cold running water for a while. Keep it there until it stops hurting. Don't put creams or soap or antiseptic on the scald. They can stop your skin from healing properly. If it's a really bad scald or burn, see a doctor.

Water makes a powerful sucking force when it goes down the drain.

TRY THIS AND SEE!

Pull out the plug and let the water run out.

GLUG!

Dangle the plug over the hole and feel the suction of the water as it tries to pull the plug down the hole.

SINKS AND PLUGS

HERE'S A COMMON SORT OF SINK . . .

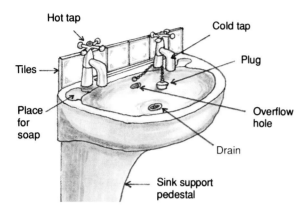

The overflow hole is there in case you leave the drain closed and tap running.

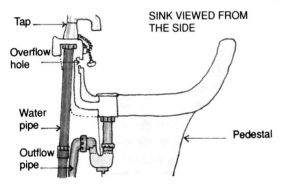

When the water level reaches the hole, water pours down the channel at the back of the sink to the outflow pipe. This stops you from flooding the bathroom.

HERE'S A PLUG AND DRAIN . . .

Drain openings are shaped the way they are so that small objects like rings can't be sucked down them.

TWO WAYS WATER CAN SWIRL

Water doesn't go straight down the drain. It swirls around first. But . . . which way does it swirl in your sink?

Check it out! Fill the sink and float a small piece of toilet paper. Open the drain and see which way around the paper goes. Can you make the water swirl the other way around? Try stirring it before you open the drain!

TAPS

THERE ARE LOTS OF TAPS.

Push-top tap

Glass-topped tap

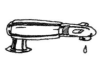

Mixer tap

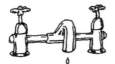

Another mixer tap

Tap for disabled people

Old-fashioned tap

TAPS WORK LIKE THIS . . .

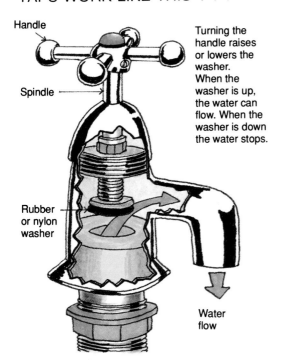

Handle

Spindle

Rubber or nylon washer

Water flow

Turning the handle raises or lowers the washer. When the washer is up, the water can flow. When the washer is down the water stops.

WHAT TO DO IF YOUR TOE GETS STUCK!

Yow!

1. If it's stuck in the cold tap, turn the tap on and the force of the water might push your toe out!
2. If it's stuck in the hot tap, don't turn the tap on. You'll scald yourself! Get some soap and squeeze a bit up into the tap. Your toe should come out!
3. If it's still stuck . . . shout for help!

A shower head is a bit like a long tap except that it has lots of small holes instead of one large one. The water shoots out of the small holes with more power than from an ordinary tap.

TRY THIS

1. Fill an old dishwashing-liquid bottle with water.

2. Squirt the water with the lid on and see how far it goes.

SSSS!

3. Now squirt it with the lid off.

FLOB!

PLUMBING

But . . . plumbing has nothing to do with plums! The name comes from an old word for lead.

The house pipes carry water to all the taps in the house.

These pipes are connected to the main pipe that brings water to the house.

Outside most houses, there's an underground tap. This is used to cut off the supply of water to the house.

If a plumber has to repair any water pipes, the water supply has to be cut off first!

THIS PLUMBER FORGOT!

HOW MUCH WOULD **YOU** PAY FOR A BATH?

BATHS $1 EACH

WATER METER FACT

In some places, the amount of water supplied to a house is measured by a meter.

People pay for the amount they use.

This encourages them not to waste it.

WHAT'S WATER WORTH?

Think what it would be like if you were lost in a hot desert with no water . . .

You'd be thirsty!

If you were dying of thirst, you'd think a glass of water was worth all the money in the world!

How much money would you give for of a glass of water?

All your pocket money? Or more?

Poor people who live in hot, dry countries often have to walk a long way to get water. That's because they can't afford to build pipes to bring it to them.

CLEAN WATER FACT

It costs a lot to make sure water is clean. There are five billion people in the world. Of these, three and a half billion can't afford clean water to drink and clean toilets to use.

Clean drinking water is valuable, so try not to waste it.

BATHROOM ODDS AND ENDS

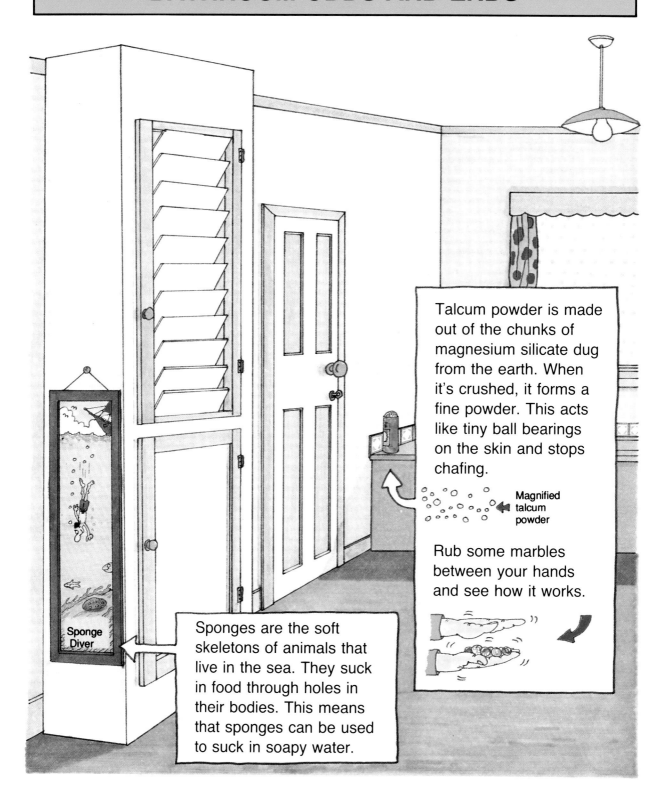

Sponge Diver

Talcum powder is made out of the chunks of magnesium silicate dug from the earth. When it's crushed, it forms a fine powder. This acts like tiny ball bearings on the skin and stops chafing.

Magnified talcum powder

Rub some marbles between your hands and see how it works.

Sponges are the soft skeletons of animals that live in the sea. They suck in food through holes in their bodies. This means that sponges can be used to suck in soapy water.

BATHROOM ODDS AND ENDS

Most houseplants grow very well in the bathroom.

Frosted glass stops people from looking in at you when you're in the bath.

Medicines should be kept safe in a locked cupboard. Get rid of old medicines. They should not be kept around the house.

Handrail helps old or disabled people to use the bath.

Loofahs are used for scrubbing backs. They are made from the large seed pods of an Egyptian plant. The pod is mashed until the skin and seeds can be removed. This leaves a fiber skeleton that sucks up water.

Diving to collect real sponges is very dangerous. Most bathroom sponges are made of plastic these days.

Some people put colored chemicals in the toilet. This makes the water look pretty, but it's bad for fish when it ends up in rivers.

TOILET TROUBLES

Everybody has to use the toilet, but lots of people think we shouldn't talk about it.

There are lots of names for toilets . . .

Can you think of any more?

Bacteria live well in toilets. They like damp places. After you've used the toilet, your hands can spread bacteria to . . .

THE PAPER

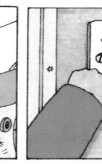

THE SEAT

THE TOILET HANDLE

THE LIGHT SWITCH

THE DOOR HANDLE

Everyone who uses the toilet can spread bacteria.

SO . . . if you don't wash, you'll spread bacteria all over the house!

STOP THE SPREAD OF BACTERIA!

Always make sure there's enough toilet paper!
Try not to miss!
Flush the bowl afterward!
Wash your hands!

TOILET TROUBLES

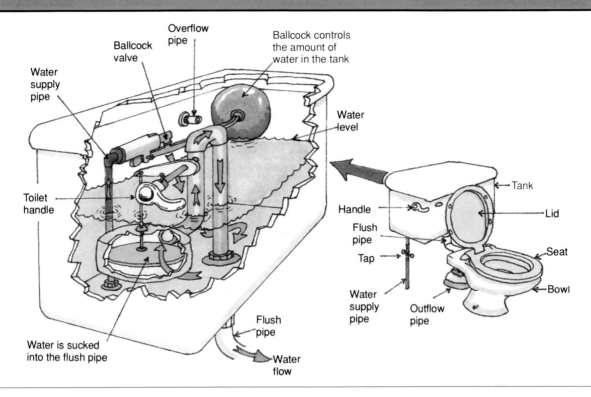

Overflow pipe

Ballcock valve

Ballcock controls the amount of water in the tank

Water supply pipe

Water level

Toilet handle

Handle

Tank

Flush pipe

Lid

Tap

Seat

Water supply pipe

Outflow pipe

Bowl

Water is sucked into the flush pipe

Flush pipe

Water flow

HOW TO UNBLOCK A TOILET

Toilets sometimes become blocked. Here are two ways to unblock them.

SLOOOSH!

Pour a bucket of water quickly down the bowl. This will often force the blockage down the hole.

If the first method doesn't work, get a plunger, which looks like this.

Ram the plunger up and down in the hole at the bottom of the bowl. It makes a great noise as well as clearing the blockage.

SCHLOOP!

SLURP!

BLUNGE!

1. First you'd go around the bend!

The bend is full of water to stop smells from coming back up the pipe.

2. Then you'd go down the toilet outflow pipe.

3. Then you'd get washed out into the sewer pipe under the road outside. Here, you'd join the waste from other people's houses. It smells terrible!

4. The small sewer pipe joins the main sewer pipe. The main pipe can be big enough to drive cars down!

5. Main sewers often have walkways so that workers can walk along and check the condition of the walls and floors.

6. Sometimes, there are dry parts where rats live. In some American cities there have been reports of alligators living in the sewers!

7. The main sewer leads to the sewage treatment plant. Here, all the sewage gets processed.

8. Finally, you'd be washed up against a grating where all the large solids are trapped. These solids are fished out every so often, so you'd be rescued at last!

9. Sewage is full of bacteria, some of which can make you ill. You'd have to go to the hospital to find out if you'd caught any diseases.

That means you'd miss . . .

WHAT HAPPENS NEXT

Sewage is made up of liquid and sludge. They are split up, and the treated liquid is pumped into the river. The dried sludge is used as fertilizer.

At certain times of the day, too much waste can flow into the sewage plant. Then it has to be pumped straight into a river or the sea. This causes pollution.

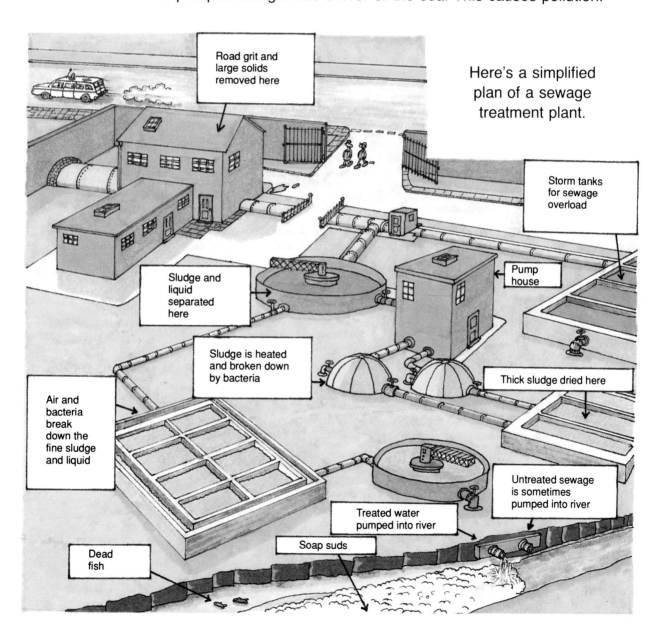

Here's a simplified plan of a sewage treatment plant.

Road grit and large solids removed here

Storm tanks for sewage overload

Pump house

Sludge and liquid separated here

Sludge is heated and broken down by bacteria

Thick sludge dried here

Air and bacteria break down the fine sludge and liquid

Untreated sewage is sometimes pumped into river

Treated water pumped into river

Soap suds

Dead fish

WATER SUPPLY

Most of our water supply comes from rivers. But rivers can become very polluted by waste from farms and factories. So rivers are dammed before they reach the polluted areas. The water collects above the dam in man-made lakes called reservoirs.

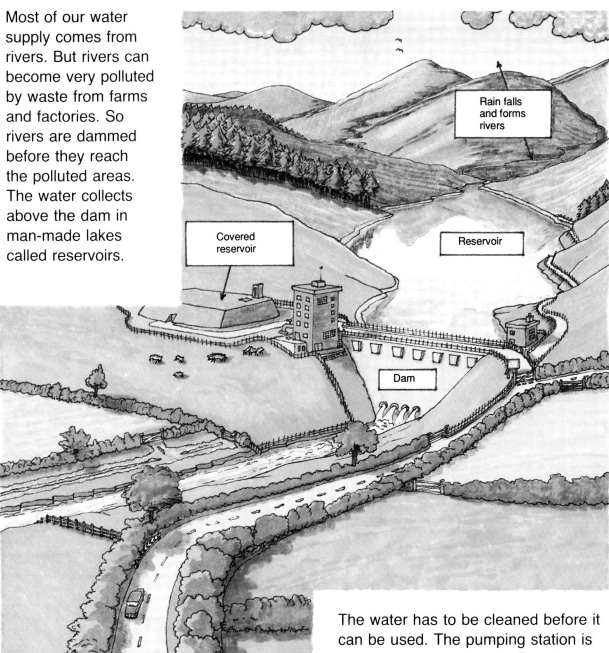

Rain falls and forms rivers

Covered reservoir

Reservoir

Dam

Reservoirs have all sorts of other uses too— sailing, fishing, and waterskiing, for example.

The water has to be cleaned before it can be used. The pumping station is also the cleaning station. The clean water is pumped into towns through the main water pipes. Sometimes the water is pumped to covered reservoirs where it is stored for later use.

UNDERGROUND RIVERS

Rivers can run underground too! Sometimes wells are drilled to pump the water to the surface.

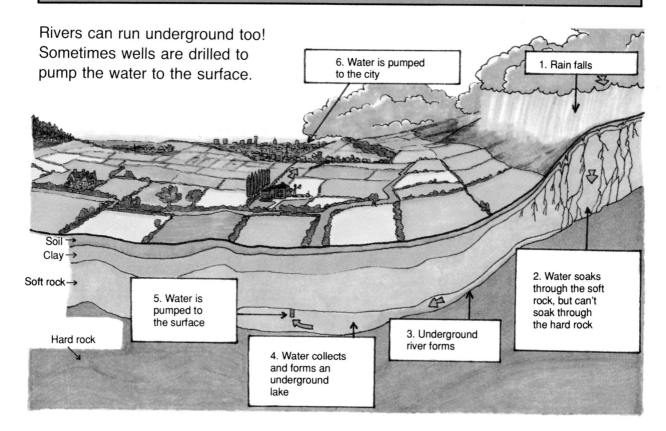

6. Water is pumped to the city

1. Rain falls

Soil →
Clay →
Soft rock →

5. Water is pumped to the surface

4. Water collects and forms an underground lake

3. Underground river forms

2. Water soaks through the soft rock, but can't soak through the hard rock

Hard rock

WELL-WISHING WATER FACT

Hundreds of years ago, people thought there were water gods living in wells. They thought they had to pay the gods so that the well wouldn't dry up. Today people still throw coins into wells and make a wish!

I wish I hadn't thrown my bus fare down there!

Underground rivers are usually much cleaner than surface rivers. That means it's worthwhile digging wells to get the water. Most rivers end up in the sea.

SAD SEAWATER FACT

Most of the Earth's surface is covered by the sea. There's enough water in the world to make all the deserts fertile. But seawater is too salty to use, and it also costs too much to take the salt out. Only about 1 quart (1 liter) of every thousand we use comes from purified seawater.

MAIN WATER PIPES

In most towns, main water pipes are laid under roads. This is because it's fairly easy to dig a hole in the road when a pipe needs to be repaired. But . . . being under the road means that pipes can be damaged by vehicles such as heavy trucks and buses.

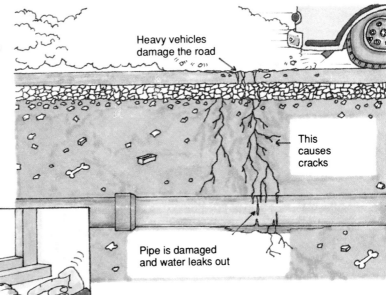

Heavy vehicles damage the road

This causes cracks

Pipe is damaged and water leaks out

Water companies keep maps that show where the pipes are. Some of the maps are very old!

But many pipes have been in the ground for so long that the maps have been lost!

If there's a leak, the pipes have to be found somehow!

It's here somewhere!

HOUSE PIPES

Most water pipes in a house or school are made of

COPPER
(for hot water)

or

PLASTIC
(for cold water and waste)

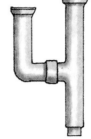

Water pipes used to be made of lead. Then it was found that lead pipes can cause lead poisoning. This damages the brain! It's thought that some Roman emperors went mad because of lead poisoning.

Some old houses still have lead pipes. If the water stays in the pipes for long enough, it can wear away the lead. Then the lead gets into the water and can cause poisoning.

If you are in a house with lead pipes, you should run the water for a few minutes before you drink any. This runs off any poisoned water that may be in the pipes.

WOTTA LOTTA HOTTA BATHS

The Romans didn't have soap, but they liked
to keep clean. They invented the Roman baths,
like this one in the city of Bath in England.

Romans often bathed together
in places similar to swimming
pools.

ROMAN NO-SOAP FACT

The Romans used to put
olive oil on their skins.
Then they scraped it off,
together with the dirt, with
a flat knife.

200 PINTS TODAY

Cleopatra was a
queen of ancient
Egypt.

It's said that she
used to bathe in
asses' milk!

She thought that
it was good for
her skin.

Some people think that mud baths are good for the skin.

But . . . you'd better find out what your parents think before you try one!

A whirlpool bath is a modern sort of bath that uses jets of air and water to massage the skin. This helps the blood in the skin to flow more easily, making the whirlpool user feel more healthy!

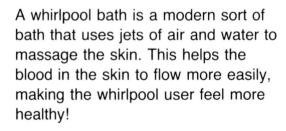

Saunas, or steam baths, are very popular in some countries.

People sit around in steamy rooms and sweat a lot!

Hot steam softens the skin and makes you sweat. The sweat pushes dirt out of your skin.

Bubble baths are great fun. But . . . if everybody used them, the sewage treatment plants would be overloaded with soap suds. Then the rivers would become polluted. Too much soap can be bad for your health!

SILLY SOAP STORIES

SOAP OPERAS

Soap operas aren't about who washes the dishes.

At one time, drama series on commercial radio and television were paid for by soap makers. They did this so that they could advertise their products during the commercial breaks.

So the shows became known as "soap operas" or "soaps"!

There's more to know about soap than how nice it smells and how it cleans your hands.

For example . . .

SOAP MAKES WATER WETTER!

If you soak some cloth in tap water, you'll see lots of little air bubbles in it. If you soak another piece of the same cloth in soapy water, there will be fewer bubbles in the cloth.

That means that the soapy water gets to more of the cloth, making it cleaner and wetter!

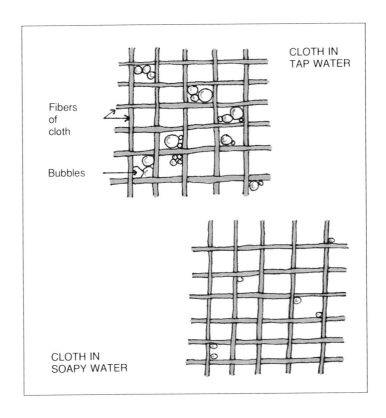

It's easy to buy a bubble maker like this from a shop. But if you want to make huge bubbles, you've got to think BIG!

1. Find a wire clothes hanger.

2. Bend it into shape.

3. Put 2 cups (about 450cc) of dishwashing liquid into a dishpan and fill the pan with water.

4. To make the bubbles last longer, add some glycerine. Ask for it at a drugstore.

5. Scoop all the foamy bubbles from the surface. Then use your giant bubble maker like this.

DIP IT IN

CATCH A FLAT BUBBLE

SLOWLY MOVE IT UP AND DOWN

TRY TO BOUNCE SMALLER BUBBLES ON YOUR GIANT BUBBLE

SHAVING

When you grow up there are even more things to do in the bathroom. Shaving, for example.

Most adults shave, even people with beards!

Some women don't like to admit that they shave. They think it's not feminine to have body hair.

Ask your mom if she shaves and see what she says. Try not to laugh too much!

Watch for bearded men and try to spot what they've had for lunch!

Beards have to be cleaned, too. They can become full of bacteria from food that falls on them!

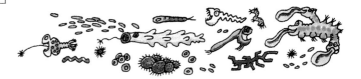

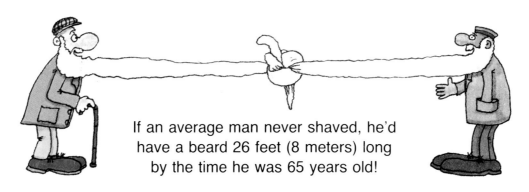

If an average man never shaved, he'd have a beard 26 feet (8 meters) long by the time he was 65 years old!

BATH TIME

Shaving takes up about fifteen minutes a day. Over a number of years, that adds up to a lot of time. The two men on page 34 have each saved about six months!

Baths and showers take up about eighteen months of an average life!

Going to the toilet takes up about six months of an average life. Think what it would be like if you could do it all at once!

All that time spent in the bathroom adds up to about two years of an average person's life. Don't waste it!

You could learn to play the piano in that time if you had a big enough bathroom!

You could get to know all sorts of amazing things. You should always have a book handy in the bathroom.

A concise encyclopedia is a good idea, so that you can read little bits at a time!

WATCH YOUR WATER!

Remember that water is valuable. Try not
to waste it when you use the bathroom.

Why not find out about water use in your house?
You'll be surprised at how much water
a household uses during a single day!

MAKE A WATER-WATCHER'S WALL CHART

WATER-WATCHER'S WALLCHART

QUARTS USED	WHEN	BY WHOM	PURPOSE
1	08.15	DAD	POT OF COFFEE
7	08.20	MOM	WASHING HANDS
7	08.22	DAD	WASHING CUPS
10	08.30	DARREN	TOILET
8	08.35	TRACEY	SHOWER
1/2	08.50	MOM	WATERING PLANTS
1/4	08.53	TRACEY	WATER FOR CAT
1/2	08.55	DARREN	WATER PISTOL

1. Find out how much water is used in a bath;
a washing machine; a toilet; a dishwashing machine.

2. Make yourself a chart like this.

3. When somebody in your house uses some
water, enter the details on the chart.

4. Before you go to bed, add up how much
water has been used.

Now that you've read this book

LEAVE IT IN THE BATHROOM!
Let other people read it too!

But
Don't let them read it
IN THE SHOWER!

FIND OUT MORE

Now that you've explored your plumbing, you may want to find out more about your water supply. Here are some books to look for in the library:

Pollution, by Geraldine Woods and Harold Woods (Franklin Watts, 1985)

The Trip of a Drip, by Vicki Cobb (Little, Brown & Co., 1986)

The Water Book: Where It Comes From & Where It Goes, by Ira M. Freeman and Sean Morrison (Random House, 1970)

INDEX